UPPER AMAZON VOYAGE BY RIVER BOAT

NORTHWATER

CONSTANTINE ISSIGHOS

Copyright 2012 © Constantine Issighos. Published in Canada. Printed in U.S.A. No part of this book may be reproduced or transmitted in any form or by any means, electronic or mechanical, including photocopying, recording, and/or by any information storage and retrieval system except by a reviewer who may quote brief passages in a review to be printed in a magazine, newspaper, or on the web without written permission in writing from the author/publisher. For information, please contact www.awaqkunabooks.com

NorthWater is an imprint of Awaqkuna Books Inc.

Vol. 1 of THE AMAZON EXPLORATION SERIES:
UPPER AMAZON VOYAGE BY RIVER BOAT

Library and Archives Canada

ISBN 978-0-9878599-0-7

Library and Archives Canada Cataloguing in Publication

ATTENTION CHILDRENS ASSOCIATIONS, BOOK STORES, PUBLIC OR PRIVATE LIBRARIES: quantity discounts are available on bulk purchases of this book series.

THE AMAZON EXPLORATION SERIES

Children's Books

by

Constantine Issighos

1   Upper Amazon Voyage by River Boat
2   The People of the River
3   The Children of the River
4   Amazon's Nature of Things
5   Echoes of Nature: a Beautiful Wild Habitat
6   The Amazon Rainforest
7   Amazonian Sisterhood
8   Amazon River Wolves
9   Amazonian Landscapes and Sunsets
10 Amazonian Canopy: the Roof of the World's Rainforest
11 Amazonian Tribes: a World of Difference
12 Birds and Butterflies of the Amazon
13 The Great Wonders of the Amazon
14 The Jaguar People
15 The Fresh Water Giants
16 The Call of the Shaman
17 Indigenous Families: Life in Harmony with Nature
18 Amazon in Peril
19 Giant Tarantulas and Centipes

My journey to the Amazon started in Lima, Peru, where I traveled by bus to the town of *Tarapoto*. Travelers going south or north into the jungle pass through the vibrant town of Tarapoto. Merchants from the interior jungle of Loreto are major suppliers of fruits and vegetables many of which are for sale in the town's open markets.

Outside Tarapoto, I walked along the riverbanks where boats were tied up, and asked every large boat owner if he were going to Iquitos, my final destination, about 350 kilometres north. No one would speak to me. They only shook their heads indicating, "No" I then asked if they knew of any boat that sailed for Iquitos, and I was pointed in the general direction of large barges— some of which were converted into passenger/general cargo boats. Still no one would speak to me. Perhaps they were suspicious of me—a foreigner—for some reason. I never found out why I was treated like this.

So far, with all the mounting little irritants, I seemed to be forgetting that my purpose for coming to the Amazon River was to learn about the riverboats, the river people's lifestyle and their resourcefulness. I bought my ticket and boarded the "Eduardo," a passenger/cargo barge that was departing in a few hours. This gave me the chance to walk around and see the local fishermen fixing their nets or selling their catch in a hustling and bustling way.

It was soon time to go back to the Eduardo, a rather ill maintained riverboat I was sharing with about 500 other passengers. Since the Eduardo provided space and food only, each passenger had to bring his own utensils, bedding and toiletries.

I assumed that as of the next morning the Eduardo would be sailing slowly for 3 days and nights, and I was hoping that the further we progressed on the Amazon the extreme heat would be reduced, and the air would become cooler. Finally, after a delay of 6 hours, we began sailing. It was a monotonous trip, with not much to do other than listen to the loud radio music or the odd child crying or laughing. It was easy to talk to people and make new friends, for as one of the few foreigners, I was the center of curiosity.

Trying to sleep in the *maca*—hammock—for the first time in my life was an unforgettable experience. Climbing into or lifting myself from it was an embarrassing task, as I kept falling off from one side or the other. Balancing was an act that I had to learn fast, as I had no other choice but to sleep on the iron deck. The food was deplorable— white rice, half of a chicken wing and a trace of something green—and the food lines were long and slow moving. There was no routine on the boat aside from at meal times. We were awakened early every day by a piercing whistle. Following meals, passengers had the rest of the day to do nothing. Most locals took to chatting; someone would always have a deck of cards to kill time. The women would huddle together to do each other's hair or nails and exchange gossip. The children played together turning the whole boat into their playground. As for the foreigners, they tended to seek each other out, exchanging stories, experiences and books.

Most of the local passengers were just traveling short distances. Along the way the Eduardo stopped in numerous small, sleepy villages wedged between the jungle and the riverbanks, in order to disembark passengers, goods and livestock. The villages varied in size but they all appeared to provide their inhabitants with very basic living conditions. As is to be expected, poor living conditions are always something hard for foreigners to see. As I kept seeing more villages sharing the same living conditions, I started to feel that aside from their poverty the people of the river were quite content and friendly. Of course, adults and children continued to be curious about foreigners.

Soon, I realized that a trip on the Amazon River by barge would depend upon how much time a person was willing to spend and the trade-off between tourist comfort on luxurious boats and going "native," travelling as most of the local people do. Most luxury riverboats are pricey, and they cater exclusively to foreigners, by provide them with comfortable cabins, large beds, private baths and air conditioning throughout. Still, I reminded myself that I was sailing the *Rio Urimaguas*—Urimaguas River— one of the Amazon's 17 great tributaries. It flows south to north from its source in the Andes to meet the main Amazon River south of Nauta. As we were crossing the river tributaries of *Paranapura* and *Huallaja*, I was lucky to be able to take pictures of spectacular sunsets, rainstorms and the Amazonian Pink Dolphins, as they swam alongside the Eduardo.

When I started my Amazon River journey, I had no idea about how vast and incomprehensible this river system would turn out to be. To tell the truth, my journey was at once magical and tedious, dangerous and mesmerizing. As we traveled for Iquitos, we passed through dangerous currents and narrow channels on pitch dark nights. Yet, where else could I watch monkeys climb through the dense foliage along the banks and observe river dolphins playing alongside the boat. I spent a lot of time on the deck taking all sorts of pictures of sunsets and of people travelling in their dugout canoes.

On clear nights, the moon was at its zenith. I could clearly pick out, along the nearest riverbanks, tangled branches,

3flamboyant flowers and large birds of all sorts. A long, motorized canoe sliced through the water, sending out a narrow wake on the otherwise perfectly smooth gray mirror of its surface. It was the time of the turn of the seasons. Soon the river waters would recede, but for the moment the riverbank trees were knee-deep in water, and I contemplated how lucky I was to be witnessing—by full moonlight—the mysterious rainforest. I scouted for night predators. I could not spot any snakes, but I spotted an eerily unmoving three-toed sloth hanging beneath the canopy and a single passive cayman—its red eyes glowing in the dark. I could feel my excitement rising, "I want to see more," my over-travelled mind said. On clear nights I could stare at the sky full of stars. Without any big city lights they were shone ever so brightly.

Within a few hours of sailing, I had left most of civilization behind. I saw only a few huts during my initial nocturnal visual exploration—tiny shacks, lit by candles or kerosene lanterns and framed by banana leaves, barely breaking the endless riverbank wall of the rainforest.

All along my river journey, I had been taking notes and pictures of boats, canoes and rafts that were held together with materials found in the jungle. Strong functional floating structures are made possible using proper techniques and ingenuity. The basic technique is notching, lashing and driving hard, wooden stakes through soft wood. For roof and sides, banana leaves are woven or just laid flat. A roof of banana branches is not only dry; it keeps the inside very cool. These drifting floating rafts are also used to transport fruits, vegetables and chickens to coastal markets. They simultaneously serve as a shelter for the driver and his family: a picture perfect Mark Twain's *Huckleberry Finn* floating raft.

Indigenous people living in villages along the riverbanks have solved their travel needs in typical Amazonian fashion—they paddle furiously as barges pass, latching their dugout canoes onto them with long hooks. Some of these paddle canoes or motorized longer ones upload fruits and vegetables destined for other markets, board or disembark passengers, and sell food and wares before setting off again, waiting to board the next barge to repeat their task.

On moonless nights, the captain has to navigate with the help of powerful spotlights pointed at the riverbanks in order to calculate shore distances and navigate narrow channels. As the Amazon River is constantly shifting, it silts on one side while cutting away on the other. No matter how high the riverbanks, the strong current of the river, in time, will erode it. This is how large trees fall into the river. Along its narrow channels there are lots of large trees anchored in the strong currents. Hitting them could punch a hole in the hull of a boat and cause large ships to sink.

My personal journey up the Amazon River and its rainforest was my deeply desired opportunity to get out of the safe routine of the tourist traveler, to be a man who achieved his expressed desire to truly experience life. I preferred to take my chances rather than stay in a civilized hotel with a sandy beach. I wanted to go and see the untouchable jungle, to travel the Amazon River as far as it would take me, and to see real animals, not someone's pets. I wanted to see the rainforest up close and personal, and experience the night jungle awakening to fulfill my heart as an adventurer.

Was I willing to step out of the safety net that civilization had built around me, to get out, touch and feel the Amazon jungle in all of its mystery, danger and wonder?

My Amazon Exploration Series of books show that I did just that: exactly what I had challenged myself to do!

AMAZONIAN RIVER BOATS

A PERSONAL JOURNEY
Yurimaguas to Iquitos

My personal journey started aboard the "Luis Eduardo" river boat. It is a steel replica of 19th century riverboats, a semi-comfortable floating vessel.

My Amazon guide Willie.

Our trip was delayed by three days. This is a typical waiting period. Boats that travel for more than 3 days on the Amazon River; seek to fill to their capacity before departure.

Leaving the main port of departure does not prevent boats from briefly stopping along the way to pick up more goods and passengers. These frequent stops often break our daily routine on board.

This is an example of goods and services transported by the "Eduardo." A truck, animals, dry goods, fresh produce and people are all sharing the same floating space.

Typical "open air" travel facilities used by local people and budget-minded foreign travellers. Lack of privacy and comfort is a bit of an inconvenience but it is a good chance to study the local people, their habits and customs, as well as their peculiarities.

Steered masterfully by the captain, "Eduardo" navigates through strong currents and treacherous upright bottom-anchored logs.

Small but fast river taxis are a common sight.

Villagers depend on the boats to transport their goods. Motorized canoes are part of the cultural links between villages.

Barges often stop to unload and load people, goods & mail. Since the river bottom is soft, barges can dock very near.

A tranquil village scene. I've taken many pictures which I share with you on the following pages.

At high tourist season, village facilities are booked for tourist, geological and scientific jungle exploration.

Out of necessity, a number of indigenous settlements are established along the complex Amazon river system. Villagers have developed the fertile flood-lands for agriculture.

I enjoy the river view and leisure moments. The boat's three levels offer an open-air walk for catching a tan, lazing with a book or conversing with a fellow traveller.

Food lines are long and slow-moving, the quality of food is poor. Passengers must bring their own utensils and toiletries.

The Amazon Exploration Series   *Constantine Issighos*

Upper Amazon Voyage by River Boat   *49*

www.ingramcontent.com/pod-product-compliance
Lightning Source LLC
Chambersburg PA
CBHW041755040426
42446CB00001B/41